BIRMINGHAM:
A LOOK BACK

Alton & Jo Douglas

New Street, 1st September 1953.

ISBN 1 85858 085 4
Published by Brewin Books, Doric House, Church Street, Studley, Warwickshire B80 7LG.
Printed by Warwick Printing Co. Ltd., Theatre Street, Warwick CV34 4DR.
Layout by Alton and Jo Douglas
4th Impression December 1998

Pat Phoenix ("Elsie Tanner" in "Coronation Street") on the balcony of the Albany Hotel,
Smallbrook Queensway, 8th April 1970.

Front cover: A typical Saturday scene in the Bull Ring, looking towards High Street, with the pillars
of the Market Hall on the left, 29th March 1948. Since the redevelopment of the sixties this is
probably the area of the "lost Birmingham" that Brummies most talk about with a great sense of
affection and loss.

BREWIN BOOKS

Doric House, Church Street
Studley, Warwickshire B80 7LG

Tel: 01527 854228 Fax: 01527 852746

Dear Nostalgic,

Over the years our most popular books have been "Memories of Birmingham" and "Birmingham Remembered" so we felt it was about time that we produced another general view of the city. No particular theme, other than a proud over-the-shoulder look at the way things were: the bustling, atmospheric Bull Ring; Lewis's – where almost anything could be bought; trams; trolleybuses; maybe even a younger version of YOU? Pore over the pictures, we'll guarantee you'll find someone or something from your past (how could we all have so many memories and yet have forgotten so much?).

Once again, magnifying glasses out, taste buds at the ready, turn the page back to yesterday and prepare to savour our city as it was.

Yours, in friendship,

Alton

Lancaster Place, February 1933. Corporation Street runs to the left and Aston Street to the right. The pub in the centre is The Swan With Two Necks. The Central Fire Station was opened in 1935, on this site. In our book, "Birmingham Remembered", at the top of page 86, we show a 1946 photograph from almost exactly the same spot.

BACK TO YESTERDAY

A fiddler and a cellist are amongst this group, who look poised to leave on an outing, outside the original Swan Hotel, Yardley, c 1890.

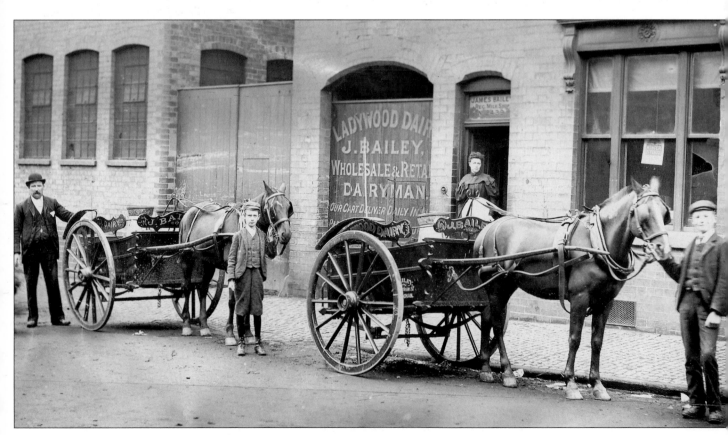

Ladywood Dairy, Sherborne Street, 1892.

Within 24 hours on September 5 and 6, 1895, Birmingham Small Arms factory produced 2,000 Lee Metford rifles which were used in the Jameson raid — the event which precipitated the Boer War.

Staff and boarders outside Soho House, Soho Avenue, Handsworth, 1894. Originally, it was the home of the industrial pioneer, Matthew Boulton, but at the time of this picture, it was in use as a girls' school. Nowadays, in the grounds of Soho House, we can find the first purpose-built community history gallery in the city.

This must be one of the most unusual photographs ever seen in our books.

A rare, panoramic, turn-of-the-century view of Corporation Street taken from the corner of New Street and Stephenson Place.

The first electric tramcar photographed at the terminus, Sutton Road, 1st March 1907.

The last time horses towed a tram, Nechells, September 1906.

Lingard Street Fire Station, Nechells, c 1907.

The Turner family of 6 Village Road, Aston, 1908. Although we usually avoid family photographs, because of their obvious limited interest, we thought this one was particularly appealing. Strangely, despite the logic of it, it comes as quite a shock to learn that the baby, Cecil, died in 1991 aged 82!

Sir,—Will you allow me to join in the protest of so many of the St. Andrew's supporters in parting with Eyre. We have been given to understand that search has been made the country over for a "class" man, and the result to date is the signing-on of one who has played but four games this season and an exchange of Eyre for Chapple. Instead of the Committee levelling up they are levelling down. It was always the same, and it appears we shall never get a "class" side at St. Andrew's. I have followed and supported the team annually for twelve years, but nothing has so disgusted me as the present action. Chelsea, Manchester United, and Newcastle pay well for players, and their supporters are proud of their team, but we are repeatedly and continually looked upon as second-raters, and I am compelled at last to succumb to the inevitable and drop my motto.

NIL DESPERANDUM.

TRAM CONDUCTORS AND CHRISTMAS BOXES.
Sir,—I, like many others, would be glad if the conductors on the Aston Trams were forbidden to annoy passengers on the cars at Christmas time by shaking collection-boxes in their faces. I travel on the cars three or four times a day all through the year, and pay legitimate fares. It is anything but pleasant to experience this every time you board a car for about a fortnight before Christmas; in fact, I prefer to walk until the fever has abated, and I know others who do likewise. I am not opposed to giving to these deserving individuals; in fact, I do each year; it is the way in which it is done that I object to. Why not have a box placed in a prominent position in the car, and allow passengers to place their mite in if they feel disposed? It is astonishing how polite the conductors are just now.—Yours, etc.,

1908 A CONSTANT PASSENGER.

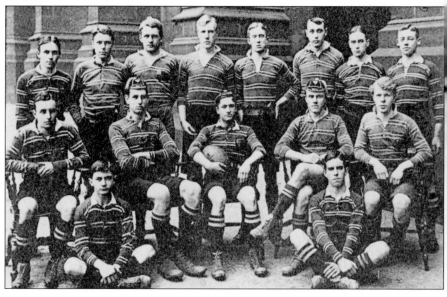

King Edward's School 1st XV, c 1908. Fourth from the right, in the back row, is J.R. Tolkien, author of "Lord of the Rings".

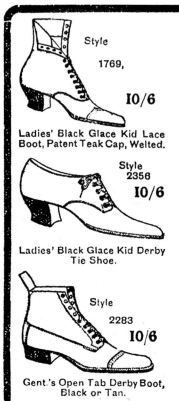

Rackhams original shop, Bull Street, 1910.

Ye Olde Saracen's Head Inn, Kings Norton Green, 1912.

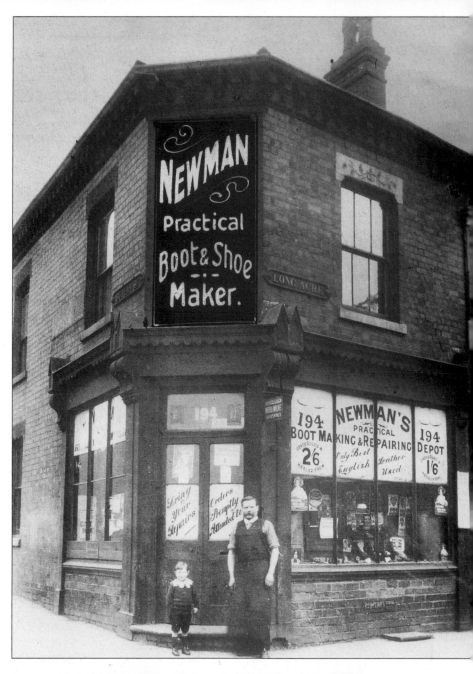

Butlin Street/Long Acre, Nechells, c 1914.
The shop was opposite Aston locomotive
sheds and continued trading until 1969,
when it was demolished as part of the
redevelopment plans.

A day in the countryside lies ahead for these trippers, The Black Horse, Park Lane, Aston, 1912.

Recruiting parade march past, GPO, Victoria Square/Hill Street, 1914, the year income tax was doubled to finance the war. Neville Chamberlain, who was an MP at the time, stands to the right of the flagpole. The following year he was made Lord Mayor and then became Prime Minister in 1937.

Drum-Head Service, Victoria Square, 1916.

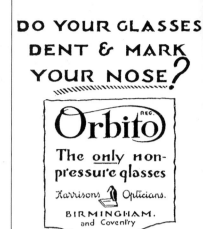

A part of the Lickey Hills, the Bilberry Hill Tea Rooms, that should be very familiar to most Brummies. Rose Hill, 1915.

Gooch Street Friends' Hall C.C., winners of the Park's Cup, 1916.

WEOLEY HILL LIMITED,

ESTATE OFFICE,

BOURNVILLE,

BIRMINGHAM.

21st February 1917.

Mr. T. Yearsley,
  c/o Mr. Winter,
    Bournville.

Dear Sir,

  We beg to inform you that we are prepared to sell you the house No.18, Witherford Way for the sum of £245. 20% must be paid before taking possession, the remainder, if desired, in ten annual instalments, interest chargeable on the balance at the rate of 4½% per annum. Cash discount of 1½% is allowed if half the purchase price is paid and 2½% if the whole amount is paid. The area of the land is approximately 370 sq.yards, and the ground rent £2 14s. 0d. per annum. Lease for 99 years from the 24th December 1914. It will be necessary to pay a deposit in order to secure the house. If a substantial amount is paid interest will be credited at the rate of 4% per annum until you take possession. Kindly let me know in writing if you wish to buy the house.

           Yours truly,

              Leonard Appleby

Chandos Road School, Sparkbrook, c 1915.

King George V and Queen Mary receive a rapturous welcome at Cadbury's, Bournville, 22nd May 1919.

1920

Five Ways, with Islington Row on the right, c 1920. The statue, in the centre, was to commemorate the industrialist and philanthropist Joseph Sturge.

Bournville Angling Club, c 1920.

Members from Bournville Friends' Meeting House, c 1920.

Entertainment on Parents' Day, Dennis Road School,
Balsall Heath, 1922.

Kings Head, Hagley Road, c 1920.

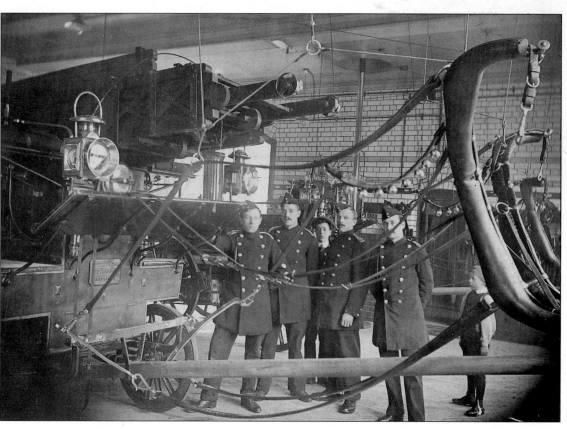

Aston Fire Station, Ettington Road, c 1922.

15

Rackhams first delivery vehicle, 1923.

Ye Olde Nelson,
Temple Row/
Bull Street,
c 1925.

FIRST BUILDING, 1774.

THEATRE ROYAL,
BIRMINGHAM.

Lessees - THE THEATRE ROYAL BIRMINGHAM LTD.
Managing Director - - - - Mr. PHILIP RODWAY.

150TH
ANNIVERSARY
CHRISTMAS EVE,
1924.

PRESENT THEATRE, 1924.

Christmas entertainment at Stirchley Infants' School,
Pershore Road, 1924.

Police Parade, Winson Green Prison, c 1925.

rom Temple Street, across Bull Street, looking
through the Minories (and the two halves of
wis's) to the Old Square, c 1926. The building
on the left-hand side was rebuilt in 1927.

5th Battalion, Royal Warwickshire Regiment, take part in their annual ceremonial parade,
with a service at St Martin's. Colmore Row, opposite Snow Hill Station, 1925.

Bull Ring, c 1926.

Bristol Street Girls' School, 1926.

Station Road Infants' School, Aston, 1928.

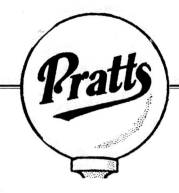

1930

King Edward's Road/Nelson Street, Ladywood, December 1930.

Wolseley Motors (1927) Ltd., Drews Lane, Ward End, 1930.

Corporation Street, from Bull Street, looking towards New Street, c 1930.

Looking from Corporation Street down Martineau Street, 1931.

Aston Lane Bridge, 1st May 1932.

Vernon Adcock, xylophonist, c 1930. He went on to become a bandleader and Birmingham's most famous "export" to Weston-super-Mare, where he completed many summer seasons with his band, mainly comprised of musicians from the city.

New Street, 1932.

Pype Hayes Nursing Home, 1932.

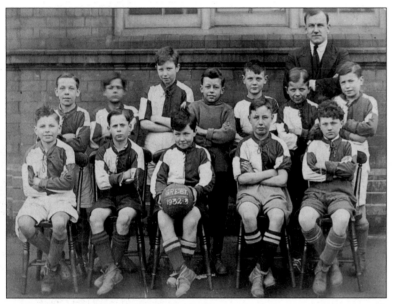

Greet Junior School F.C., Warwick Road, 1932/3.

Parents' Day, Woodhouse Road Infants' School, Harborne, 1932.

PROGRAMME
of a
RECITAL
TO CELEBRATE THE
RE-OPENING
of the
GRAND ORGAN
BIRMINGHAM TOWN HALL

IN AID OF THE

LORD MAYOR'S
DISTRESS FUND.

THURSDAY, 19th JANUARY, 1933
8 to 9-15 p.m.

A Publication of the City of Birmingham Information Bureau

ARCTIC BIRMINGHAM.

To the Editor of the Birmingham Post.

Sir,—The very interesting communication in the "Post" of Thursday last by "L. J.," entitled "Arctic Birmingham," telling of the conditions of our city area and the surrounding country in glacial times, will have whetted the appetites of some—perhaps of many—of your readers to know more.

An amateur geologist (which is all the writer of this letter can claim to be) will search with zest for every erratic boulder he may hear of and scan it with curiosity and wonder when found; but the secret of its composition and home of origin will remain a mystery. To solve this needs the trained eye of the scientific geologist, strengthened by a knowledge of mineralogy and field experience.

If any of our local professors could tell your readers where the two great boulders of basalt in Cannon Hill Park came from, the still larger and lighter-coloured boulder at the entrance of Selly Oak Park in Gibbins Lane, or the lesser one by the Ravenhurst Farm and the "Warstone," at the junction of Warstone Lane and Icknield Street, shown in the "Post" of Tuesday, January 5, it would at once enlarge our knowledge and encourage us to search further afield for these silent witnesses to the wonders of the glacial era.

Viator.

Edgbaston, January 29.

Birmingham Municipal Bank staff, Head Office, Broad Street, c 1933. This is a remarkable composite picture, made up of dozens of individual portraits, cleverly pieced together to look like a group photograph – and all done without the aid of computers!

Visiting Day, Cadbury Bros. Ltd., Bournville, c 1933.

Patrick Motors stand at the Olympia
Motor Show, 1933.

Ada Road School Choir, Small Heath, 1933.

Sir Malcolm Campbell, holder of the world land speed record, fixes the gold seal to the three millionth cycle, Hercules Cycle & Motor Co. Ltd., Britannia Works, Rocky Lane, Aston, 21st November 1933. Previously, when he had opened the new road to the British Industries Fair, it was suggested that, as the fastest man on earth, it would be amusing if he made his entrance driving a tractor, possibly the slowest vehicle on earth. He refused.

Juvenile Telephone Exhibition, 1933.

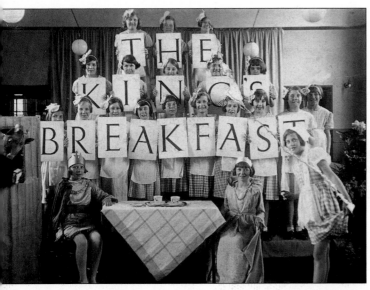

Peckham Road Senior Girls' Festival, Kingstanding, 1934.

Park Cafe, 553 Lichfield Road, Aston, c 1935.

Elmdon Airport, 1935. In April 1960 it was re-named Birmingham Airport. Today, it is known as Birmingham International Airport.

est Heath Lido, Alvechurch Road (known to locals as "The Bath Tub") shortly after its opening by singer, Gracie Fields, n 1935. It later became the home of many sections of Jarrett, Rainsford & Laughton Ltd., including Eddystone Radio. The latter moved in 1996 to Heeley Road, Selly Oak.

Cadbury's Walking Club, Lickey Hills, c 1935.

The Green, Kings Norton, c 1936. In 1938 the Kings Norton Cinema
was built on this site. It closed in 1983 and these days Grosvenor
Court, a very attractive sheltered accommodation complex, can be
found gracing the area.

Moat Farm, Common Lane, Sheldon, 1936. During the war Italian
prisoners-of-war helped to build an estate of prefabs on this site.

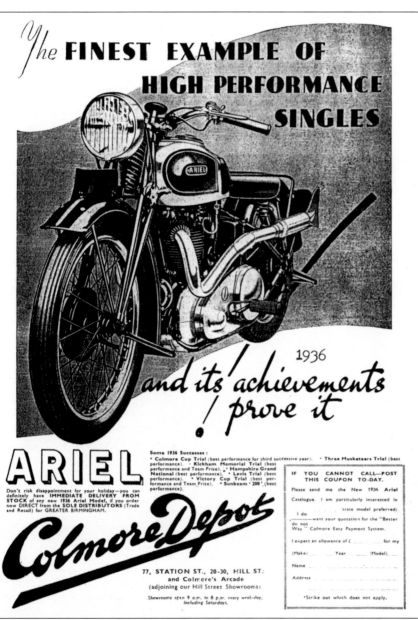

The first Wolseley Motors Ltd. Apprentices' Dinner, Farcroft Hotel, Handsworth, 14th February 1936.
Although qualification for membership ended early in 1949, when production of Wolseley cars moved from Ward End to Oxford, the Wolseley Motors Apprentices' Association still flourishes and, in fact, held its sixtieth anniversary dinner in 1996.

Inside the Waggon & Horses (prior to re-building)
Coventry Road/Wagon Lane, Sheldon, 4th February 1937.

– and from the outside.

Dorothy Ward takes time off from appearing at the Theatre Royal to tour the Business Efficiency Exhibition,
Bingley Hall, 30th September 1936. Miss Ward was the daughter of a Birmingham publican. Light comedian,
Douglas Byng, is on her left.

Harry Pell's Premiers and The Shirley Lido Revellers queue up to perform a concert at Winson Green Prison, 5th March 1937.

Co-op assistant roundsman, Harry Johnson, with Holly, Hansons Bridge Road, Pype Hayes, 1937.

Comedian, Billy Russell, goes up in the world as work goes on at Lewis's, 8th April 1937. Billy, although always thought of as a Black Country comic, was born in Birmingham. Here, he appears in his guise as "Our Bill", based on the famous Bruce Bairnsfather character, always in search of "A better 'ole". His bill matter always claimed "On behalf of the working classes". In later life he went on to star in the West End and appear in many television plays.

Coronation celebrations, George Dixon Elementary School, City Road, Rotton Park, May 1937.

Woodhouse Road School grows to such a size that two classes of older boys have to be taught in the Methodist Hall in Earls Court Road, Harborne, 1937. The teachers are Mr Powell (right) and Mr Beaumont.

Celebrating the Coronation of King George VI. Common Lane, Sheldon, May 1937.

All lit up for the opening of the Sheldon Cinema, Coventry Road, 10th October 1937.

Birmingham Corporation Tramways Car No 433 on the Alcester Lanes End/Dale End route, outside Robinsons Ltd. (furniture removal contractors) Moseley Road, Balsall Heath, 1938.

Will Fyffe, comic star of "Owd Bob", makes a personal appearance at the Gaumont Cinema, Steelhouse Lane, 18th July 1938.

Lord Nuffield (second from left) at the opening of the Morris Commercial sports pavilion, Adderley Park, 12th May 1939.

Colmore Row, with Snow Hill Station (top centre), 26th June 1939.

Soho Road, near Grove Lane, Handsworth, 14th July 1939.

Kings Heath Junior School, Wheelers Lane, 1939.

Saturday, September 2 1939

Mr. Chamberlain announced in the House of Commons that Germany's delay in replying to the British warning might be due to consideration of a proposal, put forward by Mussolini, for a Five-Power Conference.

The British and French Governments consulted on the question of a time limit for Hitler's reply.

Bill for compulsory military service between the ages of 18 and 41 passed.

Fighting in Poland increased in intensity. Warsaw was bombed six times.

Hitler sent a favourable answer to Roosevelt's appeal against bombing open towns.

British Government received pledges of support from Canada, Australia and New Zealand and from 46 Indian rulers.

Berlin officially denied that either gas or incendiary bombs had been used during raids on Polish towns.

Sunday, September 3

A final British note was presented in Berlin at 9 a.m. giving Hitler until 11 a.m. to give an undertaking to withdraw his troops from Poland.

At 11.15 Mr. Chamberlain, in a broadcast to the nation, stated that "no such undertaking had been received and that consequently this country is at war with Germany."

The French ultimatum, presented at 12.30 p.m., expired at 5 p.m.

The German reply rejected the stipulations that German troops should withdraw from Poland, and accused the British Government of forcing the war on Germany.

Fierce fighting on both Polish fronts.

A War Cabinet of nine members was created, to include Mr. Churchill as First Lord of the Admiralty.

The King broadcast a message to his peoples.

Monday, September 4.

Fleet blockade began.

In the course of an extensive reconnaissance of Northern and Western Germany during the night of September 3-4, R.A.F. aircraft dropped more than 6,000,000 copies of a note to the German people.

R.A.F. carried out an evening raid on Wilhelmshafen and Brünsbuttel. Two German battleships heavily damaged.

Heavy fighting on the Polish fronts, and the Poles claimed the recovery of several towns in the north-west, but admitted the loss of Czestochowa, near the upper Silesian frontier. More air raids over Warsaw.

France started operations on land, sea and air.

Evacuation of 650,000 children and adults from London completed.

Mr. Chamberlain broadcast a message in German to the German people in which he made it clear that Britain's quarrel is with the German régime, not with the people.

Egypt broke off diplomatic relations with Germany.

Japan decided upon neutrality.

German income tax increased 50 per cent.

Tuesday, September 5.

Warsaw admitted loss of several important towns south of the Corridor.

British aircraft carried out an extensive reconnaissance over the Ruhr and dropped more than 3,000,000 copies of the note to the German people.

President Roosevelt proclaimed American neutrality.

Jugoslavia announced her neutrality.

Argentina and Chile officially declared their neutrality.

British cargo steamer Bosnia sunk in Atlantic.

Three German ships, which might have become raiders, sunk, also in Atlantic.

WHEN THE SIRENS GO

A notice broadcast yesterday by the Lord Privy Seal's Office said:—

IN the event of threatened air raids, warnings will be given in urban areas by sirens or hooters, which will be sounded in some places by short intermittent blasts and in other places by a warbling note changing every few seconds.

The warning may also be given by short blasts on police whistles. No hooter or siren may be sounded except on the instructions of the police.

When you hear any of these sounds— TAKE SHELTER.

And do not leave your shelter until you hear the "Raiders Passed" signal, which will be given by continuously sounding the sirens or hooters for two minutes on the same note.

Fire-fighting in the early hours, Marshall & Snelgrove, New Street, 25th October 1940.

Clearing up, after parachute mines had fallen on the city the night before, Temple Row, 10th April 1941. This was the last heavy raid of the war, as far as Birmingham was concerned.

Part of B Co., 41st Warwickshire (Birmingham) Battalion Home Guard, the Bakelite Pavilion, Elmdon, September 1941.

An anti-aircraft gun on display during "Salute the Soldier" Week, Handsworth Park, June 1943.

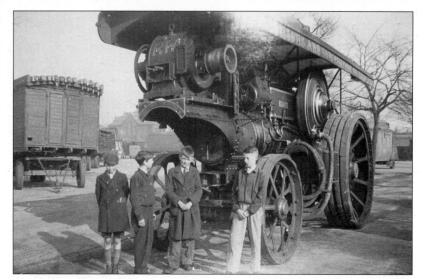

Summerfield Park, Dudley Road, Rotton Park, 1942.
The traction engine was responsible for supplying power for the dodgems and lighting in general at Robert Wilson's fun fair.

"*Thanks pal, for the way you're keeping Jerry on the run. We're backing you up by keeping in top gear with our War Savings.*"

LET'S SAVE AS HARD AS THEY FIGHT

Staff at the Corporation Omnibus Depot, Coventry Road, Bordesley, c 1944.

General Montgomery visits Wolseley Motors Ltd., Drews Lane, Ward End, February 1944. Although he is actually standing by a bren gun carrier he was there because one of his famous caravans was being refurbished at the factory. Sir Miles Thomas, Vice-Chairman of the Nuffield organisation, is on the left and next to him stands M.D., Charles Mullens.

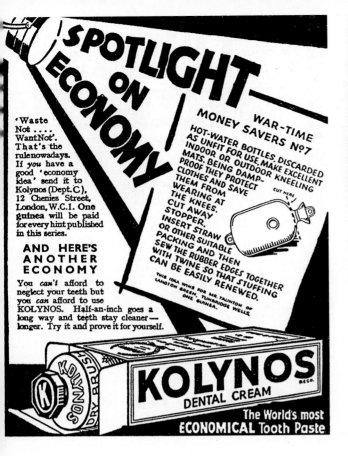

Latch and Batchelor F.C., Hay Mills, 1944/45. They were winners of the Division One Works Cup, Aston Villa Cup, Women's Hospital Cup and the Birmingham City Shield.

VICTORY 7.5.45

To-day we celebrate victory in Europe over the organised forces of evil. The Nazi regime, that "negation of God erected into a system of Government," has been destroyed by the valour and endurance and skill of freedom - loving peoples drawn from the ends of the earth. With the regime has gone German militarism and the very structure of a German State, leaving a chaotic mass of demoralised people and ruined cities in the heart of Europe. This turbulent Continent that has witnessed so many wars and the ruin of so many would-be conquerers has never before had to pay such a price for liberation from tyranny. The scene is dark indeed as a background to our relief and rejoicing. But this is not the day, at the summit and completion of an unexampled effort, to dwell on the difficulties ahead. Great as they are, they do not compare with the staggering immensity of the tasks which faced us five years ago and which we have surmounted triumphantly.

VICTORY BANDS IN BIRMINGHAM PARKS

Arrangements have been made for bands to play in the parks to-morrow afternoon and evening (at three o'clock and 6.30) as follows:—

Cannon Hill Park: Fisher and Ludlow's Band.

Handsworth Park: British Legion Band.

Aston Park: Cradley Excelsior Band.

Small Heath Park: Shirley Silver Band.

Ward End Park: Birmingham Central Band. 8.5.45

DOUBLE DEALING

Dealer in antiques: "Yes, this cake basket belonged to Queen Elizabeth."

Customer: "But it's labelled 'Birmingham.'"

Dealer: "It was presented to her by the Corporation."

TO THE PUBLIC AND LEWIS'S STAFF

•

LEWIS'S WILL RE-OPEN THURSDAY, MAY 10th at 9.30 a.m. 1945

There will be a Thanksgiving Service for the Staff at 9 a.m.

LEWIS'S, LTD., BIRMINGHAM, 4.   'Phone: CENtral 8251.

SCENES OF WORLD-WIDE REJOICING TO-DAY MARKED THE END OF THE WAR WITH JAPAN. IN EVERY ALLIED COUNTRY PEOPLE WENT WILD WITH DELIGHT. LONDON WAS WELL TO THE FORE, FOR THE DAY COINCIDED WITH THE STATE OPENING OF PARLIAMENT, AND HUGE CROWDS GAVE THE KING AND QUEEN A RAPTUROUS RECEPTION. VICTORY BELLS PEALED FROM WESTMINSTER ABBEY AND ST. PAUL'S.   14.8.45

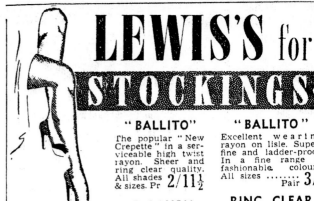

RADIO PRODUCTION EXECUTIVE,
REGENT ARCADE HOUSE,
REGENT STREET,
W.1

24th Sept. 1945.

Dear Sir,

You will probably know that, with the termination of the Japanese war, the work of this Department is completed and the Executive has now disbanded.

On behalf of the Executive, I cannot let this opportunity pass of expressing their heartfelt thanks for the splendid work done both by your Management and by your Workers in meeting their demands for Variable Condensers and several radio components.

In expanding your capacity, and also in the production of the many new types of components demanded by the Services, you were set an arduous task. But despite far more than your fair share of damage by enemy air attack, you maintained output at the highest level, and thus played an important part in the production of Radar equipment - the weapon so successful in the prosecution of the war.

I should be obliged if you would convey to your Management and to all your Workpeople the Executive's gratitude for their contribution to the final victory.

Yours faithfully,

A. A. Saunders

A.A. SAUNDERS,
Co-ordinator of Radio Production.

The Managing Director,
Messrs. Stratton & Co. Ltd.,
Alvechurch Road,
West Heath,
Birmingham, 31.

A BIRMINGHAM SOPRANO

FLORENCE Russell, a soprano of high promise, who lives at 101, Sunningdale Road, Tyseley, will broadcast for the first time on Thursday, May 10, at 8.20 a.m. in the Home Service, with the Victor Fleming Orchestra. At 17 she began studying at the Birmingham and Midland Institute School of Music and her coloratura soprano voice, with its range of two and three-quarter octaves, excited interest. In 1943 and 1944 Miss Russell won the open challenge solo in the Birmingham Estates Musical Festival.

She is a member of Hall Green Methodist Church choir, and in her radio recital will sing "The Pipes of Pan" (Monckton), "The Cuckoo" (Lehmann), "The Lass with the Delicate Air" (Arne) and "A Blackbird Singing" (Head).

TAILPIECE

HEARD in a bus. "Yes, 'er 'usband's back from the Front for good. They weren't 'alf 'aving a row last night. That, and the lights up makes you think it's peace again."

"JOY RIDERS" SET A PROBLEM

PRACTICE GROWING IN BIRMINGHAM

POLICE ASK OWNERS TO CO-OPERATE

Birmingham police are confronted with a new problem—the daily disappearance of motor cars parked in streets by their owners and later, found abandoned miles away in neighbouring counties.

The number of cases reported has jumped over 100 per cent. in the last few weeks (writes the "Mail" motoring correspondent). The police say the only remedy is the re-introduction of the war-time regulation that cars should be immobilised.

It is not suggested that cars are actually stolen — they are merely taken away without the owners' consent by irresponsible people who either want a joy ride or have missed the last bus or tram home.

In a number of cases the cars have been damaged, with the consequent serious loss to the owner, who has had to wait weeks while overworked garages do the repairs. In other cases, property had been lost from the vehicles.   16.8.45.

THE County Borough of Birmingham ranks in point of population as the third city of Great Britain. It is ideally situated close to valuable coal and iron fields, and has become a great industrial and commercial centre, with railways and canals radiating in all directions. Its pre-eminence in the manufacture of all kinds of metal ware, as well as of other products of great extent and variety, has raised it to the proud position of being the virtual capital of the English Midlands.

Standing at an average height of over 300 feet above sea level, amid healthful surroundings, 113 miles by railway N.W. of London and 90 miles S.E. of Liverpool, it has within the past few decades greatly expanded, and now embraces an area of 51,147 acres or nearly 80 square miles, with a population of 1,002,413 as returned in the Census of 1931. Latitude of Town Hall, 52° 28′ 45″ N, longitude 1° 54′ 8″ W.

Though of ancient lineage, Birmingham is essentially a modern town, gradually raised to its present high position by the wisdom and foresight of its successive civic rulers. Birmingham possesses a well-equipped **University** (with which the **Mason Science College** is now incorporated), **King Edward's School**; the Birmingham and Midland Institute, and other educational establishments; **Museum** and valuable **Art Gallery**; **Public Library**, with 24 branches; a unique **Botanical Garden**; 32 well laid out parks and 63 recreation grounds; **Golf Courses**; **Public Baths**, etc. It contains the Anglican **Cathedral of St Philip**; the interesting **St Martin's Church**; the Roman Catholic **Cathedral of St Chad**; the **Oratory of St Philip Neri**, and other ecclesiastical edifices. Other notable public buildings are the **General Hospital, Council House, Town Hall, Law Courts, Old Crown House, Chamber of Commerce, General Post Office, Memorial Hall**. There are statues to **Queen Victoria, Edward VII., Peel, Priestley, James Watt, George Dawson**, and **Josiah Mason**. The central tower of the University is a memorial to **Joseph Chamberlain**.

Gas, electricity, water, tramway, omnibus and other utility services are owned and worked by the Corporation. It has the first municipal bank in the country. Water is brought 73 miles by aqueduct from the Elan Valley in Wales.

Mitchells & Butlers "Good Honest Beer"

George Weldon conducts the "Carnival Orchestra" at the Carnival Fair, Serpentine Ground, Aston, 31st October 1946. Mr Weldon was normally seen in his official capacity as the conductor of the City of Birmingham Symphony Orchestra.

Bristol Street School, 1946.

THE TRIUMPHS and TRAGEDIES of a HOME GUARD (Factory) COMPANY

B COMPANY 41ST WARWICKSHIRE (BIRMINGHAM) BATTALION HOME GUARD

BY

MAJOR W. PERCY McGEOCH, O.C., B.COY.

(ILLUSTRATED)

Foreword by Col. J. C. PIGGOTT, C.B.E., M.C., D.L.
COMMANDING WARWICKSHIRE (BIRMINGHAM) HOME GUARD.

2/6

Profits to the Royal Warwickshire Regimental Association Benevolent Fund.

1946.

Our own comic genius, Sid Field, receives congratulatory telegrams about his "Piccadilly Hayride", Theatre Royal, 25th November 194[

Beniamino Gigli.

Ray Foxley's Levee Ramblers, one of the city's premier jazz bands, The Old Stone Cross Inn, Dale End, 1947.

George Formby and his wife Beryl take delivery of a new motorcycle, Norton Motors Ltd., Bracebridge Street, Aston, 4th July 1947. For many years, with his toothy grin and ukelele, he was Britain's favourite comedy star.

Preaching in the Bull Ring,
c 1947.

Potholes prove to be yet another hazard during the very bad
weather, Coventry Road, Small Heath (near to Muntz Street), 1947.

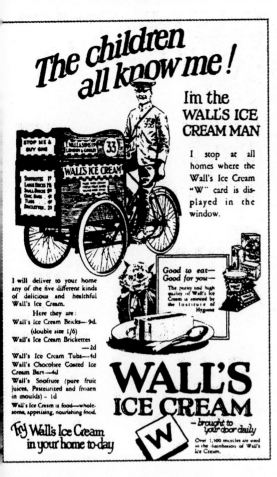

Thelma Jones meets an important guest at Gaskell & Chambers' Christmas Party, Coleshill Street, 1947.

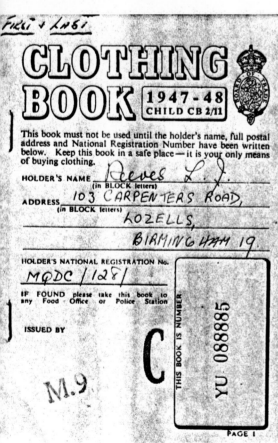

The Grail

Postcard from J. L. R. Birmingham:

It may interest your readers to know that in a book entitled "Enchanted England," by Arthur Mee, it is stated that the Holy Grail is at Selly Oak, Birmingham.

And we've a gent who says it's in a little cottage somewhere in Wales

"Random Harvest", St Paul's Dramatic Society, St Paul's Church, Lozells, c 1949.

Staff of the Customs Depot, Birmingham "Z", Sutton Coldfield, 1948.

Ike Pizzey keeps an eye out for customers, Bull Ring, 1948.

William Moss ready to take part in the May Day Parade, W.H. Moss & Son (coal merchants), Anderton Street, Ladywood, 1948.

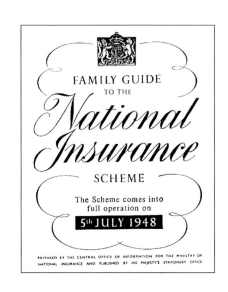
FAMILY GUIDE
TO THE
National
Insurance
SCHEME

The Scheme comes into
full operation on
5th JULY 1948

PREPARED BY THE CENTRAL OFFICE OF INFORMATION FOR THE MINISTRY OF
NATIONAL INSURANCE AND PUBLISHED BY HIS MAJESTY'S STATIONERY OFFICE

Danny Kaye, Edgbaston Golf Club, 24th June 1949. The fast-talking, scat-singing, comedy film star, after a hugely successful London Palladium appearance, did several concerts in Britain.

Great Charles Street, 1948.

A trolleybus waits at the city boundary, Coventry Road, Sheldon, 1948.

High Street, Kings Heath, with the Kingsway Cinema on the left, 1949.

Colmore Row, outside Snow Hill Station, 25th March 1949.

Corporation Street, by the Bull Street crossing, 1st July 1949.

Actor, Brian Aherne, is about to be photographed, by his wife, Alcester Road/Queensbridge Road, with the tram coming from High Street, Kings Heath, 30th September 1949. He had moved to America, in 1931, where he became the archetypal English gentleman in countless screen roles ("I Confess", "Lancelot and Guinivere", etc.). During this particular holiday he also visited his birthplace in Monyhull Hall Road, Kings Norton.

Leader of the Band

ERIC HILL.

Turning professional in 1930, after winning two individualists' awards in MELODY MAKER Contests, altoist Eric Hill founded the original Tony's Red Aces at Birmingham. He alternated between the Midlands and London before the war, and last year formed his own band and opened at the Masque Ballroom, Birmingham, where he is still resident.

LESLIE DOUGLAS TO FORM A SECOND BAND

IN an exclusive interview with a MELODY MAKER reporter, Leslie Douglas has outlined his plans for the formation of a second orchestra. This interesting news has been held up by Leslie in deference to the tragic death of trombonist Bob Lazard, but it can now be released as further proof of the consistent success of the Douglas outfit.

Resident at the Tower Ballroom, Birmingham, Leslie is inundated with requests for dates at factory dances, parties, private concerts, etc., which he cannot possibly hope to fulfil as he is fully booked at the Tower and for Sunday concerts.

BANDS BUSY 2.7.49

CURRENTLY featured at the Tower Ballroom, Edgbaston, Birmingham, and leading one of the most versatile bands in the provinces, Hedley Ward's next airing with full orchestra is on July 4 in the "Music While You Work" series, whilst the Hedley Ward Trio will be heard from the Midland Studios on July 12.

The boys' airings are gaining them a large public in the provinces, and with his concert at the Opera House, Buxton (June 24), Hedley started on a new venture in the dance-band field which looks like proving very fruitful.

Included in the outfit are no fewer than five vocalists, three of whom have broadcast as such — namely, Derek Franklyn, Jack McKechnie, and Bob Carter, who comprise the well-known Hedley Ward Trio.

The combination lines up as follows: Hedley Ward (leader and pno.); Derek Franklyn (bass); Jack McKechnie (gtr.); Bob Carter (pno.); Hughie O'Shea (drs.); Ron Adams and Eric Houghton (tpts.); Wilf Spillett (tmn.); Johnnie Hughes and Norman Jager (altos); Stan Poole and Jack Usher (tnrs.); and Gil Hazell (bar.). Hedley is very enthusiastic about his nineteen-year-old discovery, Johnny Hughes, who has only been playing sax for two years, but already shows great promise.

ROSE BEAMS

At the West End Ballroom, Sonny Rose continues to beam nightly at capacity crowds who are quick to appreciate the slick performance of Sonny's smart outfit, which, combined with clever lighting effects, makes this Birmingham spot a popular rendezvous. Fronting on alto and clarinet, Sonny Rose leads Derek Hilton (pno.), recently joined from Cab Kaye; Bob Russell (bass); Stan Pickstock (back after a spell with Cyril Stapleton), Les Coates and Stan Spencer (tpts.); Jeff Gough and Dave Raphael (altos); Dennis Jones and Norman Hill (tnrs.). Arrangements are in the hands of Dave Raphael.

Happy expressions on the faces of the Mannie Berg gang at the Grand Casino these days are due in no small measure to the pending return of bassist Sid Kay, who has been off duty since November last with a serious illness, and also to the recently announced engagement of drummer Tommy Allen to local girl Iris Cotterell.

Sharing the Casino spot is the Harry Bostock Band, soon to bid farewell to trumpet-player Tony Bourne, who joins Vincent Ladbrooke at the Isle of Man Strand Palais on July 3. Stan Upton takes over the trumpet chair.

A production of the pantomime, "Sleeping Beauty", by employees of David Powis & Son Ltd. (manufacturers of copper, brass and aluminium rivets and washers, etc.) of Golden Hillock Road, Small Heath, c 1949.

High Street, Deritend, facing towards the city centre, 24th August 1949.

1950

...edway racing, Alexandra Stadium, Perry Barr, c 1950.

LADIES SCORED MOST POINTS

It was without doubt the ladies of the company who scored most of the points when the Black Knights' Dramatic Society presented "Pride and Prejudice," by Jane Austen, at Botteville-road Hall, Acock's Green, Birmingham, last night.

This adaptation by Helen Jerome was well dressed and staged with great care. Production was by John Taylor. There will be repeat performances tonight and tomorrow. 24.2.50

DON CLARKE and his Trio are the resident group at the Airport Hotel, Birmingham, and not the Les Williams Orchestra, as was stated in a recent "MM." Both bands were among the five playing at the successful Benefit Dance for Mrs. Jim Snowdon.

Birmingham City speedway team, c 1950.

Meriden Street/Digbeth, 1950.

High Street, Deritend, 1950.

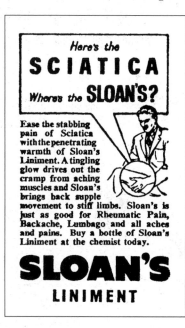

Form V, Stamford House School, City Road, Edgbaston, 1950. The teacher is Miss Horton.

Anthony Eden, Chancellor of Birmingham University, at a ceremony to bestow honorary degrees to commemorate the University's jubilee, 1950. He became Prime Minister in 1955.

Bradford Street, 1950.

"Car Park Full" notices for the Big Top site, New Street, 5th June 1950.

A fiftieth anniversary for the staff of Harrison (Birmingham) Ltd. at the Winter Gardens, Blackpool, 1950. The firm manufactured, amongst many other items, curtain hooks and rings and was based in Bradford Street.

The West Indies Touring Team, 1950.

The tram terminus, Rubery, c 1950.

WARWICK WON 3 Wkts WEST INDIES AUGUST 9 10 & 11, 1950

THE
2d. WARWICKSHIRE 2d.
COUNTY CRICKET CLUB

The Bowler at Pavilion end is indicated on big board by figure on right.
DISCS: White at 55 overs. Yellow at 60 overs. White & Yellow at 65 overs, New Ball due.
HOURS OF PLAY—First two days 11-30—7-0 p.m. Third day 11-0—4-30 p.m. with extra half-hour on third day if demanded. LUNCH 1-30—2-10 TEA INTERVAL—20 minutes.
You spoil the enjoyment of others, and indicate a lack of understanding of the Game on your own part, if you move about behind the Bowler's Arm.

WEST INDIES	1st Innings		2nd Innings	
*1 J. B. Stollmeyer	c Spooner b Grove	17	lbw b Grove	29
2 A. F. Rae	c Spooner b Grove	1	c Kardar b Pritchard	28
3 F. M. Worrell	b Grove	29	c Dollery b Pritchard	46
4 R. Marshall	c & b Grove	33	c Pritchard b Hollies	9
†5 C. L. Walcott	c Dollery b Grove	14	lbw b Hollies	41
6 K. B. Trestrail	b Grove	0	b Hollies	28
7 R. J. Christiani	c Hollies b Pritchard	4	st Spooner b Hollies	18
8 C. B. Williams	c Don Taylor b Kardar	21	lbw b Hollies	0
9 P. E. Jones	lbw b Grove	20	not out	0
10 A. L. Valentine	b Grove	5	lbw b Pritchard	1
11 L. R. Pierre	not out	0	b Hollies	0
	Extras	12		22
	Total	156		222

Umpires
H. Parks & A. Skelding
West Indies won the toss

1 wkt. for 3 2-42 3-61 4-97 5-97 6-102 7-104 8-139 9-152 10-156
1 wkt. for 63 2-66 3-94 4-113 5-174 6-214 7-214 8-219 9-220 10-222

Bowling Analysis:	O	M	R	W	Nb	Wd	O	M	R	W	Nb	Wd
Pritchard	23	6	55	1	1	–	19	5	57	3	2	–
Grove	26-4	8	38	8	–	–	35	6	69	4	–	–
Hollies	14	3	39	–	–	–	29-3	12	57	6	–	–
Kardar	10	3	12	1	–	–	3	–	14	–	–	–
Don Taylor	–	–	–	–	–	–	1	–	3	–	–	–

WARWICKSHIRE	1st Innings		2nd Innings	
1 F. C. Gardner	c Worrell b Pierre	8	hit wkt b Valentine	13
2 J. R. Thompson	c Stollmeyer b Jones	26	c Worrell b Jones	16
3 Don Taylor	c Rae b Worrell	24	not out	36
4 J. S. Ord	c Trestrail b Jones	7	lbw b Pierre	1
*5 H. E. Dollery	lbw b Valentine	3	c Jones b Valentine	0
6 A. V. Wolton	b Pierre	89	b Pierre	5
†7 R. T. Spooner	not out	66	c Walcott b Valentine	3
8 A. H. Kardar	b Jones	5	b Valentine	8
9 T. L. Pritchard	c Christiani b Valentine	15	not out	4
10 C. W. Grove	b Valentine	11		
11 W. E. Hollies	c Marshall b Valentine	6		
	Extras	24		10
	Total	284		96

Scorers:
G. C. Austin & W. Ferguson
* Capt. † Wicketkeeper

1 wkt. for 12 2-44 3-55 4-63 5-87 6-210 7-230 8-259 9-276 10-284
1 wkt. for 14 2-34 3-43 4-47 5-62 6-72 7-51 8-... 9-... 10-...

Bowling Analysis:	O	M	R	W	Nb	Wd	O	M	R	W	Nb	Wd
Pierre	15	–	57	2	1	–	5	1	17	2	–	–
Worrell	23	6	51	1	–	–						
Jones	31	10	66	3	–	–	21-4	12	33	1	–	–
Valentine	23	5	57	4	–	–	26	13	36	4	–	1
Williams	4	–	29	–	–	–						

Advertising rights acquired by the Property Publishing Company, 46, Watford Way, London, N.W.4, and printed by C. W. Towers & Son, Ltd., Stechford, B'ham, 9.

Lichfield Road, Aston, 1950.

Queueing for tickets for the Hippodrome, Inge Street, 3rd February 1951.

The Salvation Army band plays on, despite the wet conditio
Corporation Street/Cherry Street, 15th April 1951.

The Clock Garage, in its very early stages, Newport Road/Coleshill Road, 6th June 1951.

An unusual short-lived project was the creation of a helicopter station at Hay Mills Recreation Ground. Eric Williamson, who took this photograph, then boarded the Sikorski and flew to London, as a 21st birthday present, to visit the Festival of Britain. 6th July 1951.

ENGLAND v. AUSTRALIA

FOURTH SPEEDWAY TEST MATCH

(1951 Series)

ON

SATURDAY, 4th AUGUST, 1951
AT 6-30 p.m.
AT

BIRMINGHAM SPEEDWAY

BIRCHFIELD HARRIERS ALEXANDER SPORTS
GROUND, PERRY BARR, BIRMINGHAM

George Robey and his wife, along with the Rev Alfred Doyle, visit the church hall where he made his first public appearance, in 1888, St Mary and St Ambrose, Pershore Road, Edgbaston, 1951. He then went on to open the garden party in aid of church funds. The comedian was knighted in 1954.

Millpool Hill, Alcester Road South, 21st June 1951.

Smallbrook Street (with a bus travelling along Hill Street), 23rd October 1951.

Hampton Street, Newtown, 17th December 1951.

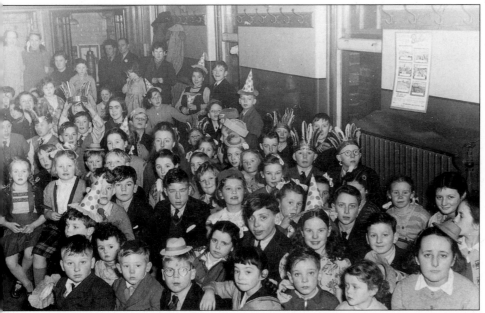

Christmas Party,
Corporation Tramway
Sheds, Rosebery
Street, Spring Hill,
1951.

Staff members take a roof-top
break, Woolworths, Bull Ring,
1952.

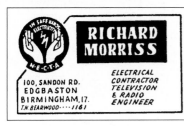

ALEXANDRA THEATRE IN PRINT

The full story of the theatre is pleasantly related by M. F. K. Fraser in "*Alexandra Theatre*," published three years ago.

This profusely illustrated book brings to life the human as well as the historical side of the "Alec" story and will revive for older playgoers many memories of people who have adorned the Alec scene in various capacities during the past half-century.

"*Alexandra Theatre*" is on sale in the Dress Circle Lounge or at Messrs. Cornish's, New Street, Birmingham, at 15/-.

High Street, Aston, 17th April 1952.

Labour politician, Aneurin "Nye" Bevan, addresses the May Day Rally, Calthorpe Park, Balsall Heath, 1952.

A break at Prestatyn Holiday Camp (later Pontin's) for employees of V. Siviter Smith & Co. Ltd. (engravers) of Moseley Street, c 1952.

Platform 5, Snow Hill Station, 30th May 1952.

Teachers and administration staff, Saltley Grammar School, Belchers Lane, 1953.

Aston Villa v Arsenal,
Villa Park, 1952.

Dudley Street/Worcester Street/Pershore Street, 29th October 1952.

Newhall Garages Ltd., Aldridge Road, Perry Barr, 1952.

On a trip to publicise her film, "Julius Caesar", Greer Garson pauses, in Chamberlain Square, to contemplate her early beginnings at the Birmingham Repertory Theatre. 9th November 1953.

A special service of prayer for the new Queen will be held at Birmingham Parish Church at 11 a.m. to-morrow. The service will be led by the Rector of Birmingham, Canon Bryan Green. It will be attended by members of the Women's Royal Army Corps and will be open to the public. The Rector states that seats will be reserved for any groups or official bodies that may wish to attend, if notice is given to him by 10 p.m. to-day.

" I feel that our tribute to the late King has been paid by the nation in the memorial services to-day," Canon Green said yesterday. "Our thoughts must now turn to the future and, with our new Queen, we must pray that we may be worthy and able to face the challenge of the years immediately ahead.

THE Duke of Edinburgh paid a two-hour visit to the British Industries Fair at Castle Bromwich yesterday. There was a " business as usual " atmosphere, for a number of overseas buyers were already in the building when the Royal visitor arrived. He showed the greatest interest in many of the exhibits and frequently displayed a wide technical knowledge.

There was an eager crowd at Stechford station when he arrived in the morning and the Duke responded with a smile to the cheering which greeted him. 1.5.53

Quite a turnout for comedienne, "Two Ton" Tessie O'Shea,
at the opening of the Singer Sewing Machine shop,
Bull Street, 18th August 1953.

Guy Mitchell is enthusiastically greeted at the
Hippodrome stage door, 10th August 1953.
The American's hit recordings included
"She Wears Red Feathers", "Sparrow in the
Treetop" and "Truly, Truly Fair".

A tram emerges from Slade Road, Erdington, en route to Steelhouse Lane, 1953. The pub is the Erdington Arms (nicknamed "The Muckman") and the area is now part of Spaghetti Junction.

The interior of a tram at Steelhouse Lane terminus, with the Wesleyan & General on the left, 1953.

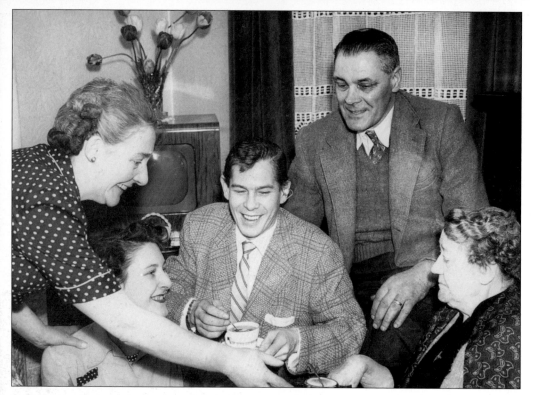

American singer, Johnnie Ray, pays a visit to the home of Sheila Hawkins (second left), president of the Birmingham Johnnie Ray Fan Club, 540 Green Lane, Small Heath, 1954. His hit-parade entries included "Cry" and "Walkin' My Baby Back Home".

Eddie Calvert, "The Man with the Golden Trumpet", signs an autograph for Kathleen Thomas of Kingstanding (check coat), Cranes, Corporation Street, 14th May 1954. His hit record was "Oh Mein Papa".

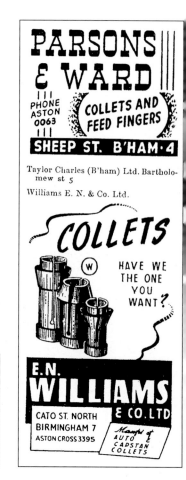

George and Dragon, Weaman Street/Steelhouse Lane, 17th May 1954.

Steelhouse Lane, 25th August 1954.

Tom Williams, Conservative candidate for Balsall Heath, in the council elections, canvasses the workforce at Alfred Davis Ltd. (Packing case manufacturers) 418/420 Moseley Road, 13th May 1954.

Mechanical problems cause a hold-up during an interview with singer, Gracie Fields (left) so husband, Boris, gets to work with a screwdriver, Queens Hotel, Stephenson Street, 1st December 1954.

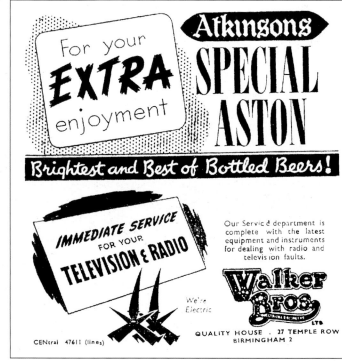

ningham Co-operative Society Ltd., Butchery
Dept., outing to the Forest of Dean, c 1955.

Eric Reeves and Len Parker take a brief break from tightening body
bolts on a milk lorry, Birmingham Co-operative Society Ltd.,
Transport Dept., Great Brook Street, Nechells, 1954.

Coventry Road, Small Heath,
2nd March 1955.

Cromwell Street/Great Lister Street,
Nechells, 1954.

Bournbrook-born singer, David Hughes, surrounded by fans, in the basement record department of Dale Forty & Co. Ltd., New Street, 1955.

Midland Red electricians' outing to London, Carlyle Works, Edgbaston, June 1955.

The Town Hall, 21st July 1955.

Loveday Street, with the Birmingham Maternity Hospital Nurses' Hostel on the left, c 1955.

Stephenson Place, 28th September 1955.

Smallbrook Street, from the Horse Fair
traffic lights, 1956.

Martineau Street, 29th February 1956.

Stan Kenton.

Film star, Fess "Davy Crockett" Parker, meets a miniature frontiersman at the Children's Hospital, 17th April 1956.

"There's Stan the Man!" Some of the six hundred fans waiting for a glimpse and possibly an autograph, as Stan Kenton makes a personal appearance at Keys Ltd., John Bright Street, 7th April 1956. The American bandleader was in Birmingham to play two sell-out concerts at the Town Hall that night.

Horse Fair/Windmill Street, 4th December 1956.

Northampton Street, Hockley, 16th January 1957.

Turfpitts Lane, Erdington, 4th July 1957.

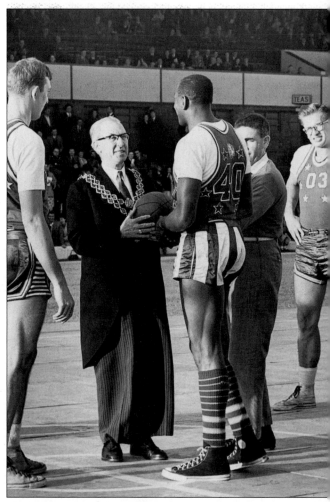

The Lord Mayor, Alderman V.J. Grogan, takes the b.. from Willie Gardner at the start of the game between world-famous Harlem Globetrotters and the United S.. Stars Basketball Club, St Andrew's, 26th July 1957.

HOME HINT

IF you are unable to release the stopper of a stone hot-water bottle, place a damp cloth over the stopper. It will then turn quite easily.

(Mrs.) N. C. SUTCLIFFE (Old Brummagenite)
Rhyl

★ UNEMPLOYMENT and short-time working were blamed for Birmingham's highest ever crime figures.

The Chief Constable, Mr. E. J. Dodd, said the city's crime figures were "out of all proportion" to the rest of the country.

SEPTEMBER 18 *1957*

THE Brummie who put Britain on two-wheels died in Cannes.

He was Sir Edmund Crane, who had built his first cycle in a back-street lean-to at Aston, Birmingham.

He and brother Harry had saved £25 for material to build their first bike in 1911. Edmund decided they needed a name to suggest strength and endurance and called it Hercules.

In their Aston factory they produced 22,000 machines in the first year — and put it up to 250,000 in five years. Knighted in 1935 Sir Edmund sold out to Tube Investments in 1947 — for a mere £3,250,000.

OCTOBER 25

WITH commercial television still a relative novelty the channel was claiming 72 per cent of the viewing time as against the B.B.C.'s 28 per cent of the 10 million who could view both channels.

A beer bottle section was just one part of the CBSO's Carol Concert rendering of Haydn's "Surprise" Symphony, Town Hall, 19th December 1957. Rifle shots and gongs also made this a concert with a difference.

Windsor Street, Vauxhall, c 1958.

Carrs Lane, 1958.

Cary Grant meets Valerie Dowen (left) from Wednesbury and Marian Davidson from Brandwood Road, Kings Heath, at a reception at the Queen's Hotel, 16th July 1958.

Lady Baden-Powell chats to some of the Wolf Cubs at the Annual Scout Rally, Handsworth Park, July 1958.

As part of a promotion for "Roses" chocolates a helicopter takes off from Cadbury's, to tour coastal resorts, during Bank Holiday weekend, 4th August 1958. Due to engine trouble it was only able to land at Weston-super-Mare and Hastings.

Harvest Festival, Delhurst Road Infants' School,
Great Barr, 17th September 1958.

The Civic Centre, as envisaged at present, will cover an area extending from the Town Hall up Broad Street to Bush House.

A civic hall is proposed, with possibly a civic theatre and a concert hall incorporated, so that combined use could be made of the restaurants and foyer. Outside, there would be a large water garden, with fountains and statues.

Further up Broad Street may be a People's Hall for meetings, a Hall of Marriage to replace the present register office—and a new site for the Midland Institute. Beyond Bush House there would be more sites available for a swimming bath big enough to take international events and for a multi-storey car park.

Another part of the scheme will contain an exhibition building with a large hall and smaller halls on a site on the West End car park. This building, it is suggested, would have two lower floors for car parks. The public would then be able to drive in, park their cars, and take the lift straight up to the exhibition hall.

The planners suggest that buildings should overlook the canal basin in Gas Street, which would be transformed into an attractive water garden.

It is suggested that buildings should be grouped round gardens.

The plan has been prepared by the City Architect, Mr. A. G. Sheppard Fidler. 5.5.58

THE MAN who built the reputation of the City of Birmingham Ochestra from 1924 to 1930 returned to the city.

Sir Adrian Boult was appointed to succeed Andrzej Panufnik as musical director and principal conductor.

He originally left Birmingham to become first conductor or the then newly formed B.B.C. Symphony Orchestra — a post which he held from the orchestra's formation until 1950.

He then acted as chief conductor of the London Philharmonic Orchestra until the end of the 1957-58 season.

A POLICEMAN stood for more than two hours outside a house in Franklin Road, King's Norton, yesterday—guarding a snake.

Fearing that the creature might be dangerous, householders had called in the police after seeing the snake in a front garden.

Eventually it was captured by a police sergeant, taken to the police station, and identified as a grass snake —and therefore harmless.

16.7.58.

Delhurst Road School, Great Barr, 1958.

Bromsgrove Street/Hurst Street, 1958. As a matter of interest the new Austin Gipsy cost £650.

Dickie Valentine opens a new stall for Ada Vickerstaff (Birmingham) Ltd., Market Hall, 14th September 1958. The singer came to prominence with the Ted Heath Orchestra but then went on to become one of the finest cabaret artists in the country.

Paradise Street/Suffolk Street, 9th June 1959.

New Inns, Muntz Street/Swanage Road, Small Heath,
5th October 1959.

For less than £500 you could buy a brand
new Mini, described as "wizardry on
wheels," with an 850c.c., air-cooled engine,
offering a top speed of 74 miles an hour
and 43 miles per gallon.

Steelhouse Lane, 21st November 1959.

Tessall Garage Ltd., Tessall Lane/Bristol Road South, 24th August 1959.

Waiting to hear the election results, Victoria Square, 8th October 1959.

Newly-elected MP for Ladywood, Victor Yates, takes a "Victory and thank you" parade along Shakespeare Road, 10th October 1959.

The January sales at C&A, Corporation Street, 4th January 1960.

Eamonn Andrews hands the big red book to Harry
Webb (founder of the Stonehouse Gang in 1938) at the
end of "This Is Your Life", 18th February 1960.

Newtown Row, with Milton Street on the left, Hockley, April 1960.

Bristol Road South, Northfield, 1960.

OF the £3,000,000 which the Minister of Education has allocated for youth service building programmes next year, the most important application lodged by Birmingham is for a mere £6,500.

And yet this application represents one of the most progressive steps ever taken in the long history of youth work in the city. It is for Ministerial grant-aid towards the cost of converting the former Bilberry Hill tea rooms at Lickey into a full-time youth leaders' training centre.   1960

Freddie Weston at work, Co-op Traffic Dept., Great Brook Street, Nechells, 1960.

Pianist-entertainer, Liberace, on a rare visit from America, finds himself in the record department of Lewis's, 4th August 1960.

Character actor/comedian, Terry Thomas, surrounded by actresses, Billie Whitelaw, Hattie Jacques, Penny Morrell and Athene Seyler at the premiere of "Make Mine Mink", Odeon, New Street, 17th July 1960.

Bull Street, 16th November 1960.

Work on the Inner Ring Road, alongside St Chad's Cathedral, c 1960. All the buildings, with the exception of the church, have now been demolished.

Under the old Bull Ring site the foundations for the new Inner Ring Road are being laid, c 1961.

Christmas dinner, Royal Exchange Assurance Co. (Birmingham Branch). Penns Hall, Sutton Coldfield, 1960.

A.B.C. TELEVISION LIMITED

cordially invite you to see

TELEVISION'S COMEDY QUIZ

"FOR LOVE OR MONEY"

at

THE TELEVISION STUDIOS . ASTON

Doors open 5-0 p.m.   No admittance after 5.15 p.m.

Saturday, 28th January, 1961   O   9

PLEASE NOTE, THE POLICE WILL NOT ALLOW THE PARKING OF CARS IN THE MAIN ROAD OUTSIDE THE STUDIOS.

ADMIT ONE   SEATS IN CIRCLE ONLY

Chamberlain Square, from a spot in Edmund Street, now occupied by the entrance to Paradise Forum, August 1961.

Tony Hancock, one of Birmingham's favourite sons, rehearses his script with the aid of a tape recorder, 15th September 1961. On 13th May 1996 Sir Harry Secombe unveiled a statue of the comedian in the Old Square.

Ashted Place, Prospect Row, 1962.

Cumberland Street/Broad Street, 1962.

The Closure Committee meet to say goodbye to four of their colleagues, Singer Motors Ltd., Coventry Road, Small Heath, c 1962.

Albert Street, 1962.

93

The Austin Motor Co. Ltd., Longbridge, c 1963.

Bull Street, 1963.

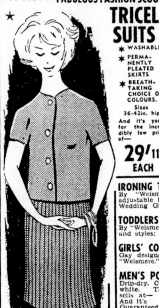

The Circle, Kingstanding, 6th June 1963.

The team from the White Hart, Aston Road, celebrate winning the Sports Argus Midland Open Darts Championship, 1963.

THE QUEEN'S visit made the new £8,000,000 Bull Ring Centre a focal point for the rapidly changing Birmingham.

And a building that was destined to be both a feature and a symbol of the new Birmingham was taking shape — and running into trouble.

In October, months after the Queen's visit, it was announced that the £1 million Rotunda, then half built, needed strengthening.

It was at a time when Birmingham was aflood with rumours that the Rotunda was developing into a "leaning tower of Pisa."

Looking down Holloway Head, as Holloway Circus is being constructed, 19th July 1963.

St John's Church of England Junior School, Ledsam Street, Ladywood, 1963.

Comedian, Tommy Trinder (in trilby) after opening the new Tesco supermarket, Coventry Road, Small Heath, 29th October 1963.

Sannazaro winning the Greyfriars Handicap, Birmingham Race Course, Bromford Bridge, 27th April 1964.

Birmingham Market, 1964.

Nechells Place/Nechells Park Road, 1964.

Well-known city busker, Reginald Cooper,
Corporation Street, 1964.

Hot baked potatoes on offer, Edgbaston Street,
3rd April 1965.

Anderton Street, Ladywood, 31st October 1964.

Queen's Hotel, Stephenson Street, 24th May 1965.

Pershore Road, Stirchley, October 1965.

Candles illuminate the gloom – because the electricity had not been connected – at the All Saints Conservative Party's area committee room, Dudley Road, Rotton Park, 18th March 1966. Incidentally, the result was just as gloomy for the Tories.

Glebe Farm Road/Swancote Road,
15th November 1966.

Members of St Andrew's Church, Oxhill Road, Handsworth, c 1966.

Cilla Black being guided across Broad Street by David Warner and director, Peter Hall (left), during the making of the film, "Work is a Four-Letter-Word", Five Ways, 1st February 1967.

Rear of 61/62 Freeth Street, Ladywood, 1966.

Rear of Alexandra Street, Ladywood, 9th June 1967.

Rear of William Street, Lozells, 5th July 1967.

Arts Director, John English, makes a point to members of the Midlands Arts Theatre Company, Studio Theatre, Cannon Hill, 13th September 1967.

E & S Brown Ltd., (manufacturing jewellers) 124 Vyse Street, Hockley, 17th November 1967.

Monument Road, with Icknield Port Road on the right, Ladywood, March 1968.

Staff of the Ministry of Pensions and National Insurance, Hamstead Hill, Handsworth, c 1968.

The Eagle Jazz Band on their way to take part in the Jazz Festival in Summerfield Park, 3rd June 1968.

Ralph Reader, with some of the cast of his "Gang Show", Hippodrome, 12th September 1968. For many years he had written and presented his scout shows but this was the first year that girls had been involved in a production. Actually, between 1965 and 1972, the name of the venue was changed to the Birmingham Theatre but this never caught on with patrons who insisted on calling it the Hippodrome!

A £5,000,000 face-lift for Birmingham Airport is planned to boost the city's claim for a major stake in Britain's air traffic.

Plans for the modernisation of the airport include a purpose-built terminal building on the far side of the present runway complex, linking it with the National Exhibition Centre, and a new railway station.

The city's new terminal — comparable with Heathrow and Manchester's Ringway — could be in operation by the end of the decade.

Detailed plans were now being drawn up for the project, Alderman Donald Lewis, Chairman of the Airport Committee revealed today.

GIANT BUILDING

He said: "A study is being carried out and we hope to be able to present details of the plans early next year."

The key to the project, he said, would be a giant terminal building sited to the east of the airport.

"We envisage one big building with plenty of room to cater for passengers," he continued.

"The National Exhibition Centre will bring extra business during the winter and the tour operators will keep the improved facilities in use during the summer."

NEW ROADS

Ald. Lewis said the new air terminal would cost £5,000,000, and the whole of the airport complex, including the question of new access roads, was being investigated by city architects.

Although Birmingham owns the land for the airport expansion, planning permission is required from Warwickshire County Council.

Yesterday, County Council's Planning Sub-Committee requested further details of the city's plans before making a decision.

Cranes Park Road, Sheldon, 1970.

Bournville Station, Bournville Lane, 27th July 1970.

MEMBERS of Birmingham City Council were today shocked by news that the city now has 750,000 square feet of shopping space standing idle—the equivalent of several hundred average size shops.

The discovery was one of the reasons why Birmingham Public Works Committee deferred for two weeks consideration of outline planning permission for the £11,000,000 redevelopment scheme for Snow Hill Station. 30.1.70

Brummies who take pride in the rebuilding of their native city may well take affront at the criticism of Birmingham voiced by a columnist in the current issue of "The Architect."

The road to Birmingham, he says, is the road to hell and nothing the Germans did in their bombing is worse than what has been done subsequently to the city.

A 14-YEAR-OLD Birmingham schoolboy will be making a solo appearance as a flautist this evening in an otherwise adult recital in the city.

Vincent Smith, of Downsfield Road, Sheldon, will be playing his flute in a programme of shorter works by Rachmaninoff, Chopin and Bach at the Royal Birmingham Society of Artists' Gallery, New Street. MARCH 1970

BIRMINGHAM shopp are saying farewel The Minories, as they h been known for gene tions, during the Spr Festival.

An the final memory The Minories is as a Sp flower garden.

The wide public thoro fare through Lewis's stor to be developed up to t storeys in a "close the operation starting month.

At ground level an ar will still allow the pu access.

"The Minories have part of the Birmingh centre shopping scene generations," said a Lev spokesman. 20.5.

A retirement gift for foreman-electrician, Sid Wilkes (dark jack Midland Red Central Works, Carlyle Road, Edgbaston, 12th December 1970.

Ted's 'ot Dog stands have been familiar all around the city for many years. Here, John Walters is the man in charge, Corporation Street/Cherry Street, 20th November 1970.

A PREPARATORY step towards the new licensing system to be introduced in gradual stages during the 70's will come with new regulations from February 1.

From that date, persons convicted of many road traffic offences and either disqualified or subject to licence endorsements must state their date of birth to the court in writing, if the court does not already know that date.

Persons pleading guilty by post to such offences will also be required to state their date of birth and sex.

The Ministry of Transport says: "This information is required by licensing authorities to help in the accurate identification of drivers convicted of road traffic offences, a facility which will be essential once those records have been centralised."

DEBUT FOR THE CITY OF BIRMINGHAM LIFEBOAT

THE £70,000 lifeboat that Birmingham helped send to sea answered its first emergency call early today.

Lifeboatmen at Exmouth were alerted when a 20ft. sloop was reported overdue on passage from Weymouth to Exmouth.

Within minutes, the City of Birmingham lifeboat, delivered for duty at Exmouth two weeks ago, was pounding through a heavy swell.

Weymouth lifeboat was also alerted.

After an hour, the City of Birmingham, helped by a Shell tanker anchored in Torbay, spotted the sloop at Lyme Bay, near Sidmouth.

The tanker made a 30-mile scan with radar to help pinpoint the sloop Mayfly, with a crew of two.

There were fears for the Mayfly when she vanished after being spotted off Portland Bill last night.

She was towed to Exmouth by the City of Birmingham.

● The lifeboat will be officially named at a ceremony in Exmouth in May, 17 months after Alderman Charles Simpson, then Birmingham's Lord Mayor, launched his £40,000 appeal for the vessel. *1970*

Joseph Lucas Ltd. ran a scheme to encourage employees' suggestions for work improvement. Maurice Tedd, second left, receives a cheque for £1,000, Great King Street, 1970.

New lease of life for clubs, theatre

IT was generally accepted in the city today that Birmingham faces a challenge with the provision of entertaining in its new role as the country's exhibition centre.

"The city must now take two leaps forward," said Mr. R. Caldicott, the city's Festival Officer, who is also this year's president of the Institute of Municipal Entertainment.

"We must start thinking like seaside resorts and yet go one stage further. The resorts plan their activities on a local basis.

"Birmingham must now think and act internationally."

The first major show business reaction to the proposed exhibition centre was a strong hint that the Birmingham Theatre will be given a new lease of life.

The second was that the Castaways Theatre Club, closed last year because of financial difficulties, may be reopened under a new management.

There will, I understand, be a statement about the club's future shortly.

With these developments, speculation heightened about the future of another night club "casualty," the Penguin Club at Aston, which also closed last year.

With the more positive line about the Birmingham Theatre came the offer, too, that it could be used as a centre within a centre for business conferences.

Reindeer gift to city 1970

A FURTHER link between the people of Finland and Birmingham was forged today with a gift of a pair of reindeer.

The reindeer, 18-months-old and as yet unnamed, were presented to the Lord Mayor and Lady Mayoress of Birmingham, Alderman and Mrs. Stanley Bleyer, by the Deputy Mayor of Helsinki, Mr. Gunnar Smeds.

The handing-over ceremony took place in the presence of the Mayor and Mayoress of Dudley, Alderman and Mrs. J. Rowley, at Dudley Zoo, where the reindeer, a male and female, have been in quarantine.

The animals, which have yet to grow spread antlers, are to remain at the zoo for 12 months to comply with quarantine regulations and will then be transferred to Birmingham children's zoo in Cannon Hill Park.

Members of the Ladies Circle in the panelled dining-room, Aston Hall, 26th June 1971.

The opening of the Aston Expressway, 1st May 1972.

The team from the Sunday afternoon ATV programme, "The Golden Shot", transmitted from Birmingham – Alan Bailey ("Bernie the Bolt"), Anne Aston (hostess), Wally Malston (scriptwriter), Bob Monkhouse (host) and Mike Lloyd (producer/director), 7th October 1971. On 17th June 1973, when the then-host, Norman Vaughan, lost his voice, the show was taken over by Alton, who had been the warm-up comic for over five years.

THE white bull terrier that was top dog at Cruft's, comes of Birmingham's own breed.

A Kennel Club spokesman says: "We have no record of a white bull terrier winning the Cruft's supreme championship before."

The breed was evolved in the middle of the last century by Mr. James Hinks, whose grandson, Mr. Carleton Hinks, was until recently still occupying the old family "Canine Repository" in Sherlock Street. 1971

Kolhapur, the former LMS Jubilee-class locomotive, hauls train enthusiasts past visitors to the Standard Gauge Steam Trust's open day, Tyseley, 11th June 1972.

Maurice Chevalier, in the person of Bob Martin, takes a curtain call at the staff Christmas party, British Home Stores, New Street, 1973.

Gem Street School, Aston, 1973.

Aldridge Road, Perry Barr, 1973.

Cliff Richard in town to film the musical,
"Take Me High", New Street, 1973.

Botanical Gardens, Edgbaston, 30th May 1974.

"Sports Argus" darts correspondent, Bill Bailey, receives a retirement gift from the paper's team, 22nd June 1974.

Bill Webster (centre right) celebrates his retirement, Lucas Aerospace Ltd., Shaftmoor Lane, 1975.

CHARLIE DRAKE, the entertainer, is also an accomplished artist.

He is seen here with his painting entitled "1984" at the opening of the Euro Arts and Crafts exhibition Bingley Hall, Birmingham.

He has staged several one-man exhibitions and is a respected figure in the art world.

The exhibition, the first of its kind in Britain, includes paintings, pottery, sculptures, graphics, metalwork and photography.

The total value of exhibits on show is put at well over £250,000.

The most spectacular is the work of Mr. Rowland Lindup, senior artist at Blackpool pleasure beach. He can be seen working on a 100 foot canvas, depicting 100 top comedians who have appeared at the resort over the last century.

Other craftsmen display their skills and there is £1,000 worth of prizes in each of six groups. The exhibition, which continues until March 25, is open to both amateurs and professionals. 18.3.76

Comedian, Larry Grayson, gets to grips with four models, after opening the Birmingham Motor Show, Bingley Hall, 10th April 1976.

Perrott's Folly, Waterworks Road, 7th January 1977.

Italian opera maestro, Tito Gobbi, catches up on his correspondence before he embarks on a series of master classes for young professional singers, Grand Hotel, 4th December 1977.

World Cup football has an impact on the pupils of St Michael's Junior and Infants' School, as they dress in the national costumes of the teams, Bartley Green, 17th June 1978.

Bugatti racing cars line up during the "Birmingham welcomes the Motor Car" display, St Martin's Lane, 7th October 1978. These particular entrants commemorated the winning of the first "round the houses" grand prix, by a Bugatti, in Monaco in 1929.

High Street, Sutton Coldfield,
23rd April 1979.

A converted double-decker bus serves as a story-teller's den, as Jayne Mills reads to children from Reddicap School,
8th May 1979. Sutton Coldfield Children's Library hired the bus as its contribution to "National Tell a Story" week.

Local artist, Phyllis Hindle, shows her painting of the Great Stone
Inn, Church Road, to Arthur Radburn, Manager of the
Birmingham Municipal TSB Bank, Northfield, 1979. The bank
held an exhibition of her pictures.

The city's leading show business publicist and agent, George Bartram, surrounded by photographs of his clients,
Gas Street, 2nd August 1979.

119

1980

Bennett's Hill looking towards New Street, 6th February 1981. In our book, "Birmingham at War Vol 1", on page 69, we can see the same area but with bomb-damaged buildings all around.

Hollywood star, Stewart Granger, meets the fans and signs copies of his autobiography, "Sparks Fly Upwards", Hudsons, New Street, 12th February 1981.

The Rag Market, Bull Ring, 1981.

A farewell chord from Helena Walker as she retires after 35 years of playing for adult education classes, Clock Tower Centre, High Street, Harborne, 2nd April 1982.

As one of many educational trips, held in the area, children from Weoley Hill playscheme gather at Sarehole Mill, Moseley, 3rd September 1982.

Vintage buses on parade at the West Midlands' Vintage Vehicle Society's fifth annual rally, Cannon Hill Park, 19th September 1982.

Noelle Gordon, star of the ATV soap-opera, "Crossroads", says goodbye to some of her dresses worn in the programme and now donates them to the Church of England Children's Society Shop, College Road, Handsworth Wood, 22nd July 1981.

Civic heads from all over the Midlands attend a dinner at Highbury Hall, hosted by the Lord Mayor and Lady Mayoress of Birmingham, Denis and Mollie Martineau, 28th April 1987.

Park Hill Primary School's prize-winning float in the Moseley Festival Carnival Parade, 27th June 1987.

After giving out prizes in the sale raffle, comedienne, Marti Caine, poses with winners, Frank Griffiths (left) from Nearmoor Road, Shard End and Ian Harrison from Manchester. Lewis's, 8th January 1985.

Evening Mail salesman, Brian Shaw, gives away free drinks to customers who buy the VE Day 40th anniversary souvenir supplement. Bull Ring outdoor

Teachers and pupils from Fairfax School, Sutton Coldfield, 22nd March 1983. The school held the UK record for the most Duke of Edinburgh awards gained by pupils at any school (2,265).

The Earl of Bradford restrains radio/TV personality, Nicholas Parsons, as he tries to test-drive a rather damp car, Icknield Port Road depot, 24th January 1990. It was the launch of a clean-up of the canal system organised by British Waterways and the Tidy Britain Group.

American film star, Raquel Welch, appears at the Alexandra Theatre in George Bernard Shaw's "The Millionairess", April 1995.

CITY OF BIRMINGHAM SYMPHONY ORCHESTRA

The Lord Mayor, Coun. Fred Grattidge, launches the "Readathon" at Pegasus Junior and Infants' School, Castle Vale, 29th March 1988.

Rubery Youth Marching Band serenade Kelly Ann Ronan, Victoria Common, Northfield Carnival, 1st July 1989.

Just some of the stars attending the Four Theatres Ball, Albany Hotel, 7th January 1988. Dora Bryan ("Charlie Girl", Hippodrome), Peter Goodright and Maggie Moone ("Dick Whittington", Alexandra Theatre), Max Boyce ("Jack and the Beanstalk", Grand Theatre, Wolverhampton) and Sue Devaney ("Wizard of Oz", Repertory Theatre).

Equally famous as a singer and chairman of Watford FC, Elton John, along with former Sports Minister, Denis Howell, signs a petition against the Government's proposed football membership scheme, St Andrew's, 21st January 1989.

The Lord Mayor, Coun. J.R. Balmer, urges the crowd to throw coins into the fountain to raise funds for charity, Chamberlain Square, 14th April 1955. In the background Mason College can be seen, in Edmund Street.

ACKNOWLEDGEMENTS
(for providing photographs, for encouragement and numerous other favours)

Geoff Allen; The late Stanley Arnold; Bob Bailey; Norman Bailey; Cliff Baker; Barbara Ball; Bob Bill; The Birmingham City Council Dept. of Planning and Architecture; The Birmingham Post and Mail Ltd; Nell Blackburn; Jim Boulton; Colin Bragg; Ron Butler; Dave and Kath Carpenter; Evelyn Chapman; Al & Beryl Cooke; Alan and Brenda Cronshaw; Veronica Davies; Eddystone Radio Ltd.; Margery Elvins; Tony Felmingham; Eve Francis; The Royal Regt. of Fusiliers, St John's House, Warwick; Bill Harrison; Pat Hessel; Barrie Hickman; Robert Houghton; Anne Jennings; A.H. Johnson; Alan and Jean Johnson; Harry Johnson; Dave, Thelma and Tom Jones; Lyn Kennedy; John Landon; George Leaman; Eric Leyser; Barry Littleford; Sylvia Manton; Gordon Matthews; Millie Mills; Pete Monckton; Dennis Moore; Cliff Newman; Rose Norris; William Orton; Harold Parsons; George Peace; Arthur Radburn, Shirley Rae; Eric Reeves; Mary Robertson; Norman Rogers; Keith Shakespeare; Maureen Silcocks; Kath and Charles Smee; Soho House; Maurice Tedd; Bob and Joan Wilkes; Rosemary Wilkes; Eric Williamson; Sandra Williamson; Wolseley Motors Apprentices' Association.

Please forgive any possible omissions. Every effort has been made to include all organisations and individuals involved in the book.

Back Cover: Looking towards the city, Salford Bridge, at the junction of Lichfield Road, Gravelly Hill, Tyburn Road and Slade Road, 28th August 1950. This area is now part of Spaghetti Junction.

As part of the Birmingham International Jazz Festival, Trevor Whiting and his Jazz Swingtet attract attention in the Great Western Arcade, 4th July 1987.

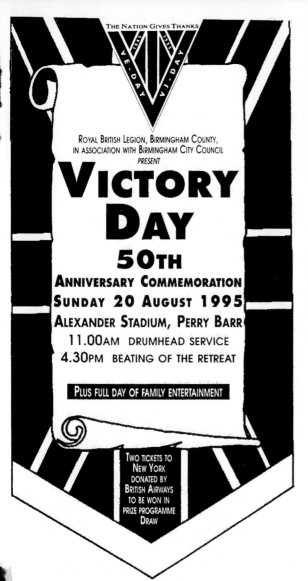

ROYAL BRITISH LEGION, BIRMINGHAM COUNTY,
IN ASSOCIATION WITH BIRMINGHAM CITY COUNCIL
PRESENT

VICTORY DAY

50TH

ANNIVERSARY COMMEMORATION

SUNDAY 20 AUGUST 1995

ALEXANDER STADIUM, PERRY BARR

11.00AM DRUMHEAD SERVICE
4.30PM BEATING OF THE RETREAT

PLUS FULL DAY OF FAMILY ENTERTAINMENT

TWO TICKETS TO
NEW YORK
DONATED BY
BRITISH AIRWAYS
TO BE WON IN
PRIZE PROGRAMME
DRAW

A Lanchester, built in 1901, drives out of MBC Metal Powders, as part of a centenary rally, Montgomery Street, Sparkbrook, September 1995. All Lanchester cars, built from 1895, passed through this door.

JEWELLERY QUARTER
DISCOVERY CENTRE

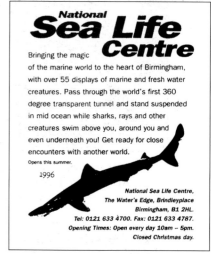